REPTILES

Sarah Wilkes

WORLD ALMANAC® LIBRARY

Please visit our web site at: www.worldalmanaclibrary.com
For a free color catalog describing World Almanac® Library's list of high-quality books
and multimedia programs, call 1-800-848-2928 (USA) or 1-800-387-3178 (Canada).
World Almanac® Library's fax: (414) 332-3567.

Library of Congress Cataloging-in-Publication Data

Wilkes, Sarah, 1964-
    Reptiles / by Sarah Wilkes.
        p. cm. — (World Almanac Library of the animal kingdom)
    Includes bibliographical references and index.
    ISBN 0-8368-6213-9 (lib. bdg.)
    1. Reptiles—Juvenile literature. I. Title.
    QL644.2.W592   2006
    597.9—dc22   2005052632

This North American edition first published in 2006 by
World Almanac® Library
A Member of the WRC Media Family of Companies
330 West Olive Street, Suite 100
Milwaukee, WI 53212 USA

This U.S. edition copyright © 2006 by World Almanac® Library. Original edition
copyright © 2006 by Hodder Wayland. First published in 2006 by Hodder Wayland, an
imprint of Hodder Children's Books, a division of Hodder Headline Limited, 338 Euston
Road, London NW1 3BH, U.K.

Subject Consultant: Jane Mainwaring, Natural History Museum
Editor: Polly Goodman
Designer: Tim Mayer
Illustrator: Jackie Harland
Picture research: Morgan Interactive Ltd and Victoria Coombs
World Almanac® Library art direction: Tammy West
World Almanac® Library editor: Carol Ryback
World Almanac® Library cover design: Jenni Gaylord

Photo credits: (t) top; b (bottom); l (left); right (r).
Cover photograph: eye of an iguana.
Title page (clockwise from top left): a mangrove snake; Jackson's chameleon;
Morelet's crocodile; Pacific turtle hatchling.
Chapter borders (from top to bottom): macro photographs of the skins of a Nile crocodile,
an emerald tree boa, a rattlesnake, and a marine iguana.
CORBIS: / Bryan F. Peterson cover. Ecoscene: / Reinhard Dirscheri 7(b), 8; / Jack
Milchanowski 9; / Wayne Lawler 10; / Jack Milchanowski 17; / Clive Druett 22; / Robert
Pickett 28; / Reinhard Dirscheri 35; / Alexandra Elliott Jones 43. naturepl.com: / Doug
Wechsler 4; / Steven David Miller 5, 26; / Jurgen Freund 7(t), 11(t); / Michael Durham
11(b); / Pete Oxford 12; / Mike Wilkes 14; / Tony Phelps 15, 33; / Nick Garbutt 16, 29;
/ George McCarthy 18; / Mark Carwardine 19; / Mary McDonald 20; / Brandon Cole 21;
/ John Cancalosi 23; / Michael Pitts 25; / Bruce Davidson 24, 27, 38, 42; / Robert Valentic
30; / Barry Mansell 31; / David Kjaer 32; / William Osborn 34; / Anup Shah 36, 37, 39, 40;
/ Hermann Brehm 41.

Printed in China

1 2 3 4 5 6 7 8 9 10 09 08 07 06

CONTENTS

It is not possible to include information about every reptile species in this book. A taxonomic chart for reptiles appears on page 44.

WHAT ARE REPTILES?

Hundreds of millions of years ago, reptiles ruled Earth—dinosaurs on the land, pterosaurs in the air, and plesiosaurs in the oceans. Most became extinct about sixty-five million years ago, but some survived. Today, about seventy-eight hundred species of reptiles, including snakes, lizards, turtles, and crocodiles, roam Earth.

Reptilian features

All reptiles share certain features and characteristics. Their body is covered in a continuous layer of scales that forms their leathery skin. These scales are different from the individual scales covering the bodies of fish. Reptiles' scaly skin reduces water loss and enables reptiles to survive in desert habitats. Like amphibians and birds, reptiles have a single bone in their middle ear, whereas mammals have three. Unlike mammals, the lower jaw bone of reptiles consists of a series of bones instead of a single jawbone.

Scales covering snakes such as this mangrove snake (*Boiga dendrophila*) vary in size. Larger scales appear on the underside of the body; smaller scales appear on the upper surface.

All reptiles are ectothermic, or cold-blooded, which means their body temperature is similar to their surroundings. They gain and lose heat by altering their behavior. For example, many reptiles bask in the Sun to warm up their bodies or move into the shade or water to cool down. Although reptiles do not use energy to regulate their body temperature and can survive on much less food than similar-sized mammals, this characteristic also limits their range of habitats. In colder regions, reptiles become inactive during the winter months.

CLASSIFICATION

Biologists have identified several million different organisms. They group together those with shared characteristics. The classification system moves through general to specific categories until each organism receives an exact binomial classification: a "last" name—the genus—and a "first"name—the species. The animal kingdom is divided into phyla (singular: phylum). Each phylum is divided into classes, which are divided into orders, and then into families, genera (singular: genus), and species. A genus and species names a single organism that differs from all other organisms. In most cases, only members of the same species can reproduce with each other to produce fertile offspring.

The classification of the Nile crocodile (*Crocodylus niloticus*) is shown on the right.

KINGDOM: Animal

PHYLUM: Chordata

CLASS: Reptilia

ORDER: Crocodylia

FAMILY: Crocodylidae

GENUS: *Crocodylus*

SPECIES: *niloticus* (Nile crocodile)

Use the first letter of each word in this sentence to remember the classification order:
Kings **P**lay **C**hess **O**n **F**ridays, **G**enerally **S**peaking.

Life cycle

Most reptiles lay eggs that hatch into miniature versions of the adult animal. Reptilian eggs have a leathery shell that protects the embryo inside and stops it from drying out. Some reptiles give birth to live young.

Classification

Reptiles are a class of vertebrates, along with fish, amphibians, and mammals. The class is divided into four orders: turtles and tortoises; lizards and snakes; tuatara; and crocodiles and alligators. This book covers reptilian orders and some families and examines the way each group has adapted to its environment.

This young Florida red-bellied turtle (*Pseudemys nelsoni*) has just hatched from its egg. It already is recognizable as a turtle and will grow steadily throughout its life.

TURTLES AND TORTOISES (TESTUDINATA)

Turtles and tortoises are an ancient order of reptiles. They live in most temperate and tropical regions, on land and in the ocean. The order Testudinata contains almost three hundred species, including tortoises, terrapins, and turtles.

Shared features

Turtles and tortoises are the only vertebrates with a bony shell. This unique feature is formed from the rib cage and part of the backbone. Turtles and tortoises have an unusual anatomy because their pectoral and pelvic girdles (their shoulders and hips) are positioned within their rib cage. Instead of teeth, they have a horny, toothless beak. They have five digits on each foot.

Shell armor

The shell consists of two parts containing fifty to sixty bones. The upper, often domed, part is called the carapace. It covers the back. The lower part, the plastron, covers the abdomen and front of the chest. A bony bridge joins the two parts of the shell along the sides. The shell offers protection from predators and often provides camouflage. Turtles and

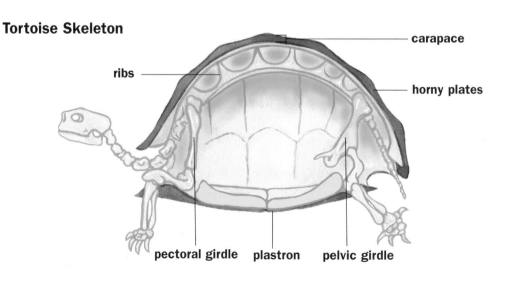

Tortoise Skeleton

ribs — carapace — horny plates — pectoral girdle — plastron — pelvic girdle

tortoises can withdraw their heads inside the shells. The dome-shaped shells are particularly difficult for predators to crush in their jaws. Not all carapaces are dome-shaped. Some tortoises have a relatively flat carapace so they can squeeze into rock crevices, while turtles adapted to living in water have flat, streamlined carapaces to help them swim.

The Hermann's tortoise (*Testudo hermanni*) is a straight-necked tortoise. When threatened, it pulls its head straight back inside its shell.

Classification

The order Testudinata is divided into two suborders, Peurodira (side-necked) and Cryptodira (straight-necked), according to how the tortoise or turtle draws its head into its shell. Straight-necked tortoises and turtles pull their heads straight back into the shell. Side-necked tortoises and turtles have longer necks, so they tuck their necks sideways into the shell's opening.

KEY CHARACTERISTICS
TESTUDINATA
- **Bony shell made up of a carapace and plastron.**
- **Horny, toothless beak.**
- **Five digits on each foot.**

What's the difference?

Tortoises are terrestrial animals. Their shell is covered by horny scales. Their forelimbs are heavy with flattened, unwebbed toes. Turtles are mostly aquatic, although they do pull themselves out onto land. They tend to have a flatter shell, and their toes are joined together by webbing. Turtles use their forelimbs like flippers or paddles for swimming.

Turtles, such as these green turtles (*Chelonia mydas*), swim long distances. Their flat shell slips easily through the water.

Living in water

Unlike most other reptiles, turtles spend much of their lives in and around water. Their bodies have adapted to their aquatic habitat. Turtles have lungs, not gills like fish, so they must come to the surface to breathe. They have various adaptations, such as being able to absorb oxygen through the lining of their throat, that help them increase the amount of time they can stay underwater. Some turtles have a very slow metabolism. They burn the energy from food slowly and do not need much oxygen. For instance, loggerhead musk turtles can survive underwater for hours or even days. Their metabolism is so slow that they absorb all the oxygen they need through their skin. These turtles also can survive in water with low levels of oxygen, such as muddy channels. Turtles have flattened, paddle-like front limbs that help them swim.

Hawksbill turtles (*Eretmochelys imbricata*) live on coral reefs, where they feed on the coral, breaking off large chunks. They also eat sponges, seaweeds, jellyfish, crustaceans, and small fish.

The alligator snapping turtle (*Macroclemys temminick*) wiggles a small, red, wormlike projection at the end of its tongue (visible here) to attract small fish.

Food and hunting

Most tortoises are herbivores. They feed on a range of plant foods, including leaves and fruits. The majority of turtles and terrapins are omnivores. They feed on a variety of plant and animal foods, such as corals, jellyfish, worms, and mollusks. Since they are not fast-moving predators, they prey on slow-moving animals. They hunt by waiting for prey to pass, relying on camouflage to stay hidden. When the prey comes into range, they strike. Some turtles and terrapins feed on tiny animals in the water using a sucking technique. They open their mouth and expand their throat at the same time, creating a vacuum that sucks in water and food.

Surviving the cold and heat

Like all reptiles, turtles and tortoises can survive extreme cold and heat by entering a metabolic state called estivation, which is somewhat like hibernation. Their body temperature drops more than normal, and their metabolism slows considerably so that they need little oxygen or food to survive. Desert tortoises and turtles estivate during the hottest periods of the year. Tortoises and turtles that live in colder parts of the world, such as spotted turtles in North America, creep into a hole or cave during the winter months.

SPOTTED TURTLES

Spotted turtles of North America spend winters sleeping in large groups of up to twenty-three individuals on the bottom of shallow rivers, ponds, and lakes that often freeze over. In the spring, the turtles emerge from the river and pond beds and spend much of the summer on land. In late October or early November, they return to the water for the winter.

Turtle life cycle

Like most reptiles, turtles and tortoises lay eggs. They lay large clutches of thirty to fifty eggs, so that at least some will survive. The adults do not tend to their eggs or their hatchlings. Most tortoises live between forty and sixty years, and some live much longer.

Marine turtles live pelagic lives, swimming across the oceans in search of food. When they are ready to breed, the adults swim back to traditional breeding beaches—a journey that can cover thousands of miles (kilometers)—to mate. Then at high tide, when the water reaches far up the beach, the females pull themselves onto the beach to lay their eggs. Each female digs a hole into which she lays about one hundred eggs before covering them with sand and leaving. The females may lay several clutches during the breeding season. The young turtles hatch between fifty and sixty days later. They use an "egg tooth" on the tip of their beak to break out of their shell before scampering frantically to the water. The large number of emerging turtle hatchlings attracts predators, such as lizards and birds. Only a few hatchlings make it to the ocean alive.

A female loggerhead turtle (*Caretta caretta*) has pulled herself onto the beach to lay her eggs. Most turtles come ashore under the cover of darkness to lay their eggs in the sand.

GALÁPAGOS GIANT TORTOISES

Galápagos giant tortoises (*Geochelone nigra*) live in the Galápagos Islands 620 miles (1,000 kilometers) off the coast of Ecuador. These giant tortoises can grow up to 4 feet (1.3 m) long and weigh up to 550 pounds (250 kilograms). Many live for more than one hundred years. Galápagos giant tortoises do not mature sexually until they are twenty to twenty-five years old. Compared with most tortoises, the birthrate of Galápagos giant tortoises is extremely low. Females lay two to sixteen eggs in each clutch. They hatch four to eight months later.

A female turtle digs a deep hole using her hind legs and lays her eggs before covering the nest with sand to protect the eggs from predators. The entire egg-laying process takes no more than three hours.

Tortoise life cycle

Most tortoises mate and lay their eggs in the spring. Some species lay up to one hundred eggs in a hole in the ground, while others lay them under leaves. The young tortoises hatch between sixty and one hundred twenty days later, depending on the species.

Temperature and sex

Scientists discovered that the temperatures surrounding the eggs influence the sex of reptiles before they hatch. At a certain temperature, approximately equal numbers of males and females hatch, but if the temperature rises or falls slightly, more of one sex will hatch. In turtles and tortoises, if the temperature falls slightly, more males emerge, and if it rises by a couple of degrees, more females hatch.

A Pacific pond turtle hatchling (*Clemmys marmorata*) breaks out of its shell. All the eggs in a turtle clutch hatch at the same time.

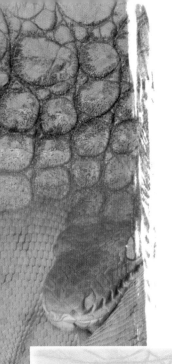

TUATARAS (RHYNCHOCEPHALIA)

Tuataras are the only remaining relatives of a group of ancient reptiles that lived more than two hundred million years ago. They survived after most of the dinosaurs died out. Today, tuataras are found only on thirty islands off the coast of New Zealand.

Tuataras belong to the order Rhynchocephalia, which has just one family containing two species. The name *tuatara* means "old spiny back" in the Maori language—used by some native people in New Zealand—in reference to the spiny necks and heads of these reptiles.

KEY CHARACTERISTICS
RHYNCHOCEPHALIA

- Two pairs of skull arches (a type of cheek bone under the eye).
- Abdominal ribs.
- Each rib has an uncinate process.
- Jawbones have serrated edges that form teeth.
- "Third eye" connected to the brain.

Shared features

Each of the tuatara's ribs has a small, bony projection, called an uncinate process, at its back edge. This process forms a link between adjacent ribs and strengthens the entire rib cage. Tuataras' teeth are unusual because they are part of the jawbone instead of separate structures. Tuataras do not grow replacement teeth, so the oldest tuataras are virtually toothless. They chew their food between smooth jawbones. Unlike other reptiles, tuataras also lack an eardrum and a middle ear.

Tuataras have a "third eye" on top of their head that is connected to their brain. The third eye has a lens and a retina, but it is not actually involved with sight. Scientists believe tuataras use this light-sensitive organ to control the amount of time they spend basking in the Sun. The third eye is visible only in hatchlings, when it has a translucent patch over the top. In adults, it is covered by their scaly skin.

Tuataras live in underground burrows, either digging their own or living in those made by burrowing seabirds. They are nocturnal (active at night) and feed on insects, earthworms, and snails. They may also eat small lizards, amphibians, and young seabirds.

Life cycle

Tuataras reproduce only once every three to four years. They usually mate in the summer (January in the Southern Hemisphere), but they do not lay eggs until the following summer. The female tuatara lays between six and fifteen eggs in a nest. They hatch in twelve to sixteen months.

ENDANGERED

Tuataras once were widespread in New Zealand, but today they are considered endangered. In the mid-nineteenth century, they were hunted by people for food. Then rats arrived on settlers' ships from Europe. The rats ate the tuataras' eggs and killed their young. Today, tuataras live on only a few islands that have rocky shores, making them inaccessible to people and "exotic" animals—animals that are not native to an area or habitat.

Tuataras are more active at lower temperatures than most other reptiles, and their body temperature ranges from 43 to 56 °Fahrenheit (6 to 13 °Celsius), which is usually lower than their surroundings. The low temperatures cause them to grow slowly. Female tuataras cannot breed until they are about twenty years old. Adults may live for more than one hundred years.

Tuataras (*Sphenodon* sp.) are stout animals with a thick tail. Adults can grow up to 30 inches (80 centimeters) long and weigh less than 2.2 pounds (1 kg).

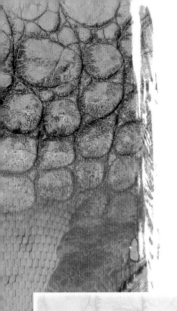

SNAKES (SERPENTES)

Snakes are legless reptiles. They are highly efficient, carnivorous predators, and one of the few groups of animals in which every member is a carnivore. Snakes are found worldwide except for the polar regions, Iceland, Ireland, New Zealand, and other islands.

KEY CHARACTERISTICS
SERPENTES

- Legless.
- No movable eyelids.
- No external ears.
- Large number of vertebrae in their backbone.

Snakes belong to the order Squamata, along with lizards (*see page 44*). The snakes are placed in their own suborder, Serpentes. There are about twenty-seven hundred different species of snakes, including the adder, boa, python, cobra, grass snake, and garter snake.

Snake features

The main feature of snakes is their lack of limbs. They also lack movable eyelids. Instead, snakes have transparent eyelids that are fused to form a special transparent scale, called the spectacle scale. Snakes lack external ears, but their sense of hearing is acute. Their ear bone is attached to their lower jaw and picks up vibrations and low-frequency noises. Their other senses, such as smell, also are well-developed. Some snakes have specialized sense organs not seen in other vertebrates, such as the heat-sensitive pits of the pit vipers (*see page 23*), and the Jacobson's organ in the roof of the mouth that is used for tasting. Snakes test the taste of objects by flicking their tongue and bringing the taste sensation into the Jacobson's organ.

Snakes, like this grass snake, shed, or molt, their worn-out skin. Molting also gets rid of parasites, such as mites and ticks. During its molt, the snake usually hides and stops eating. It can be unusually aggressive during molting.

A snake's body shape is an adaptation to its lifestyle. Burrowing snakes tend to be shorter, with a thick body and short tail, while climbing snakes generally are longer and thinner. A single row of large, wide scales on their underside helps most snakes grip the ground, while the scales on their upper body surface tend to be smaller. Most snakes have more than one hundred twenty vertebrae in their backbone, but some species have as many as five hundred eighty-five vertebrae. Those with more vertebrae have stronger and more flexible spines. Snakes' internal organs are elongated to fit into their long body. Paired organs, such as the lungs and kidneys, are arranged so that one lies above the other.

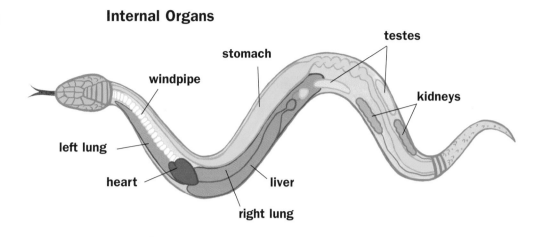

Internal Organs

testes

stomach

windpipe

kidneys

left lung

heart

liver

right lung

Life cycle

Most snakes lay leathery eggs in a nest and give little parental care. Young snakes break out of the egg using an egg tooth. Once hatched, they slither into the undergrowth to escape predators.

Classification

The suborder Serpentes is divided into three infraorders: blindsnakes, primitive snakes, and advanced snakes. The infraorders contain a total of eighteen families. Five of these—boas, pythons, vipers, colubrids, and elapids—are featured on pages 16 to 23.

Some snakes give birth to live young. The young develop in soft egg membranes inside the female's body. They break open the membrane soon after birth. This newborn smooth snake (*Coronella austriaca*) is still in its membrane.

BOAS AND PYTHONS (BOIDAE AND PYTHONIDAE)

Boas and pythons are constricting snakes that squeeze their prey to death. They include some of the largest snakes in the world. Both boas and pythons are found in Africa, Australia and Asia, while boas also live in North and South America and Madagascar.

Boas and pythons are two families in the primitive snakes infraorder. The boa family consists of twenty-eight species, including the boa constrictor and rubber boa. The python family contains approximately twenty-five species, including the reticulated and rock pythons.

Shared features

Boas and pythons are characterized by a skull that is heavier than that of other snakes. Their jaw has an extra bone called the coronoid. These snakes have a pelvic girdle (hips), a feature that has been lost by other snake species through evolution. Boas and pythons also exhibit remnants of back limbs that appear as spurs. The spurs are more visible in male snakes, near the tail. Unlike snakes in the advanced snakes infraorder (*see pages 18 to 23*), boas and pythons have two lungs positioned one above the other in the body. Some boas and pythons have heat-sensitive pits in their jaws to help them detect prey.

This Madagascar boa constrictor (*Acrantophis madagascariensis*) has caught and wrapped its body around a lizard. The boa will swallow the lizard head first.

16

Killing prey

Boas and pythons kill by coiling their heavy body around a prey animal, for example, a deer, and squeezing. The coils get tighter as the prey animal struggles. After it suffocates its prey, the snake relaxes the coils and starts swallowing the animal whole, head first. Its lower jaw unhinges and swings open to swallow large prey. The jaws on either side work alternately—gradually "walking" the body into the mouth. Once swallowed, the prey is slowly digested.

Getting around

Tree boas' long body is adapted for living in trees. They have a prehensile tail that wraps around branches and helps them move remarkably quickly from tree to tree. They move by extending their head out from one branch to another, gripping firmly with their long prehensile tail. Most tree boas rest coiled up around a branch with their head hanging down, ready to catch any passing prey.

The tree boa (*Corallus enydris*) is a nocturnal snake found in the rain forests of Central and South America.

Life cycle

Boas and pythons lay eggs. Female pythons wrap their body around their eggs to keep them at the right temperature. If the temperature drops, they shiver to produce heat, which warms up the eggs. Female pythons guard their eggs to protect them from predators until they hatch. The larger snakes have a life span of up to forty years.

COLUBRIDS (COLUBRIDAE)

The family Colubridae belongs to the infraorder of advanced snakes. This is a huge and varied family of about sixteen hundred species, including the garter, grass, corn, snail-eating, kingsnake, and milk snake. They are found worldwide except in the polar regions and the northernmost parts of North America and Asia.

Shared features

All colubrids lack a functioning left lung. Unlike the boas and pythons, colubrids do not have a pelvic girdle or any remnants of hind limbs, nor do they have a coronoid bone in their jaw. Colubrids have a jaw that is even more flexible than the constrictors because the upper and lower jaws are not connected to each other. Most colubrids have a distinct head and tapering body. The burrowing species are exceptions—they are streamlined with no distinct neck between the head and the short body. Most colubrids have large, plate-like scales on their head.

This grass snake (*Natrix natrix*) has opened its jaws wide in order to swallow a toad. The toad has inflated its body to make itself look bigger than it really is and to make it more difficult to be swallowed.

Hunting

Colubrids use a variety of hunting and killing methods. Many are fast-moving diurnal (day) hunters, but some are nocturnal species, too, such as the mangrove snake and kingsnake. Some species constrict their prey, while others use venom (poison). Colubrids have solid fangs. Their venom travels along a groove on the surface of the fang into the wounded prey.

Garter snakes are diurnal. They hunt during the day using their sight, hearing (sensing ground vibrations), taste, and smell. Garters are agile and move along the ground quickly. In contrast, the mangrove snake rarely leaves the trees. It is a nocturnal snake that moves through the trees with grace and speed. When not hunting, the mangrove snake curls up and spends the day motionless.

Surviving the cold

Snakes cannot cope with the cold climate of northern latitudes, so they survive by sheltering underground and estivating through the winter. For example, North American garter snakes crawl into large holes and caves, where they pile up together to reduce heat loss. When temperatures rise again in spring, they emerge together.

KEY CHARACTERISTICS
COLUBRIDAE

- No functioning left lung.
- No pelvic spurs visible and no remnants of pelvic girdle.
- No coronoid bone in jaw.

The mangrove snake (*Boiga dendrophila*) is a nocturnal predator that relies on its sense of hearing and smell to find prey.

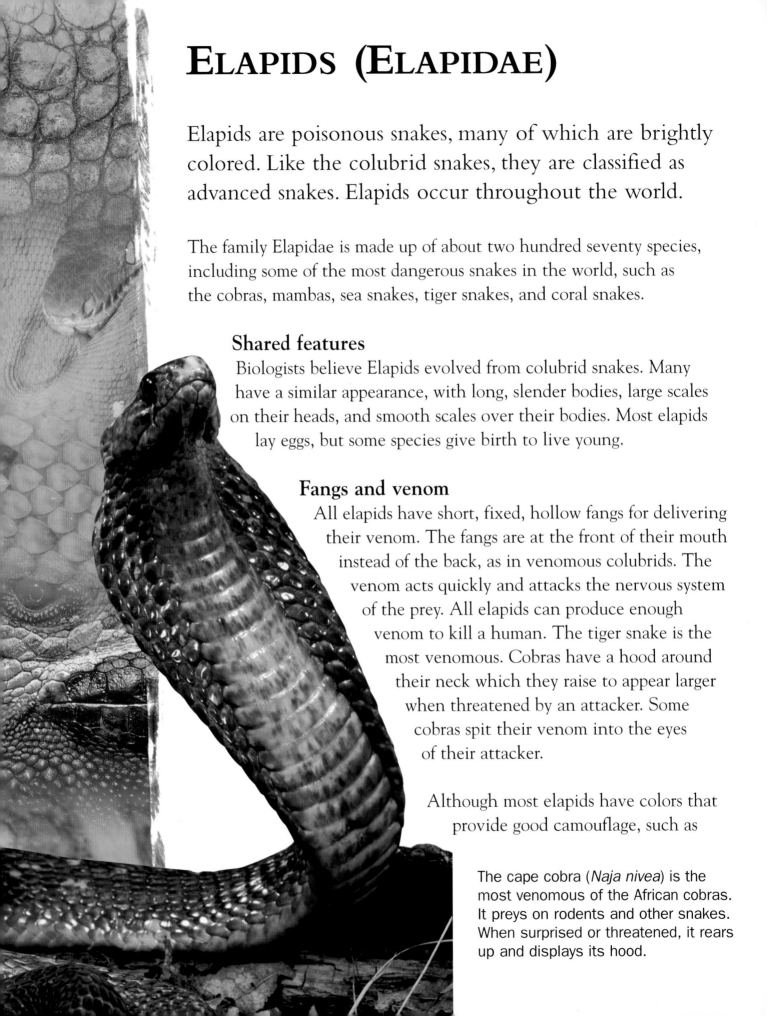

ELAPIDS (ELAPIDAE)

Elapids are poisonous snakes, many of which are brightly colored. Like the colubrid snakes, they are classified as advanced snakes. Elapids occur throughout the world.

The family Elapidae is made up of about two hundred seventy species, including some of the most dangerous snakes in the world, such as the cobras, mambas, sea snakes, tiger snakes, and coral snakes.

Shared features

Biologists believe Elapids evolved from colubrid snakes. Many have a similar appearance, with long, slender bodies, large scales on their heads, and smooth scales over their bodies. Most elapids lay eggs, but some species give birth to live young.

Fangs and venom

All elapids have short, fixed, hollow fangs for delivering their venom. The fangs are at the front of their mouth instead of the back, as in venomous colubrids. The venom acts quickly and attacks the nervous system of the prey. All elapids can produce enough venom to kill a human. The tiger snake is the most venomous. Cobras have a hood around their neck which they raise to appear larger when threatened by an attacker. Some cobras spit their venom into the eyes of their attacker.

Although most elapids have colors that provide good camouflage, such as

The cape cobra (*Naja nivea*) is the most venomous of the African cobras. It preys on rodents and other snakes. When surprised or threatened, it rears up and displays its hood.

shades of green and brown, the coral snakes have red and black warning colors. Coral snakes are small snakes that spend much of their time underground, feeding primarily on other snakes. In spite of their small size, their venom is extremely poisonous.

Living in water

Most elapids are terrestrial (live on land), but a number are arboreal (live in trees), and some burrow in the ground. Sea kraits and sea snakes are aquatic—adapted to life in the ocean. They have flattened tails for swimming and nostrils that close when underwater. These snakes give birth to live young in the ocean. Sea kraits live in the ocean but come ashore to lay their eggs. Sea snakes and sea kraits feed mainly on fish, which they kill and eat quickly before the fish sink to the ocean floor.

Sea kraits such as this one (*Laticauda* sp.) are excellent swimmers. They breathe air and must close their nostrils when they dive to avoid a nose full of water.

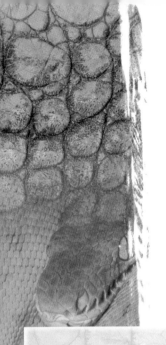

VIPERS (VIPERIDAE)

The poisonous Viper family is considered the most highly evolved of all the snakes. They belong to the advanced snakes (Caeophidia). The roughly two hundred thirty species include the pit viper, adder, Gabon viper, and sidewinder. Vipers are found the farthest north and south of the equator than any other snakes.

KEY CHARACTERISTICS
VIPERIDAE
- Long, hollow fangs.
- Triangular-shaped head.
- Give birth to live young.

Shared features

Vipers have long, hollow fangs that fold against the roof of the mouth when not in use. Their bodies range in length from about 10 inches (25 cm) to just under 13 feet (4 meters). Their distinctive, triangular-shaped head accommodates their fangs and the muscles of the venom glands. Vipers have rough scales. Their heads are covered with small scales, and their eyes have vertical pupils. They usually have camouflage coloration. Most give birth to live young.

The poison of vipers works differently from that of the elapids. It attacks the tissues and blood. The Russell's viper—found in Pakistan and across Southeast Asia—is responsible for more human deaths than any other poisonous snake.

Gabon vipers (*Bitis gabonica*) have the longest fangs of any snake, measuring up to 1.5 inches (4 cm) long. These snakes are well camouflaged among dead leaves on the ground.

Sidewinders

Most snakes move across the ground by throwing their body into a series of curves and pushing against the ground. Others glide forward in a straight line. Sidewinders have a unique method of moving that developed as an adaptation to crossing hot sand deserts. As they move sideways, only a couple of parts of their body contact the ground at any one time. This prevents the snake's abdomen from resting on the hot sand for too long. Sidewinding snakes leave an S-shaped trail in the sand.

Pit vipers

A pair of heat-sensing pits between the eyes and nostrils of pit vipers allows them to hunt at night. The sensors detect temperature differences between objects and their surroundings. They help pinpoint the location of mammals and birds at night. Some pit vipers also use their sensors to find cool places to shelter themselves from high daytime temperatures.

Rattlesnakes

Rattlesnakes shake the rattle at the end of their tail to scare off predators. The rattle consists of dried scales. With every molt, the snake sheds its skin, leaving an enlarged scale (rattle) at the end of its tail.

Rattlesnakes, such as this Arizona black rattlesnake (*Crotalus viridis cerberus*), shake their rattle to warn animals to stay away. Biologists believe that rattlesnakes developed their rattle because it made a louder noise than the sound of their tail shaken against dry vegetation.

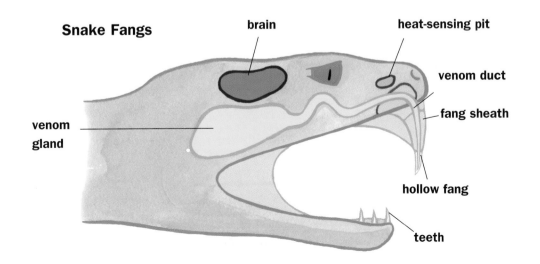

Snake Fangs

brain

heat-sensing pit

venom duct

fang sheath

venom gland

hollow fang

teeth

The delivery of venom works somewhat like a hypodermic needle. As the snake's fangs bite down, they squeeze muscles on the venom gland, forcing the venom through the duct in the fang and out into the victim's wound.

23

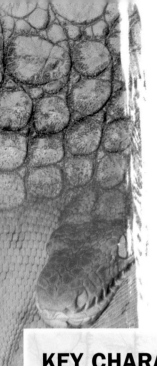

LIZARDS (LACERTILIA)

Lizards are a large, successful group of reptiles. They live all over the globe as far north as Canada and as far south as the tip of South America.

Lizards belong to the same order as snakes: Squamata. They form the suborder Lacertilia. It contains about forty-five hundred species of lizards, including geckos, monitors, skinks, chameleons, and iguanas.

KEY CHARACTERISTICS
LACERTILIA

- Most have a "fragile" tail.
- External ear opening.
- Movable eyelids.
- Long tongue.
- "Third eye" connected to the brain.

Shared features

The obvious difference between lizards and snakes is that most lizards have four limbs. They hold their limbs out at right angles to their bodies, so that when they walk, their bodies sway from side to side with their long tail swinging behind. Lizards have small, sharp teeth along the edges of their jaws. Their teeth fall out and are replaced frequently. Lizards have an external ear opening and eyelids that

This Jackson's chameleon (*Chamaeleo jacksonii*) belongs to the superfamily Iguania, which includes chameleons and iguanas. Jackson's chameleon has a particularly thick, scaly skin.

can open and close. Their tongue is long and can extend beyond their mouth to catch prey. Like tuataras, lizards have a light-sensitive area at the top of their head called the "third eye" that is connected to their brain (*see page 12*).

Losing their tail

Many lizards voluntarily shed their tail when threatened or caught by a predator. This ability is called "autotomy." It allows the lizard to escape while the predator watches the tail thrash around on the ground. Most lizards can shed their tails because they have a "fragile" tail—a tail with a weak joint between two vertebrae. After it has been shed, the tail regrows.

Scales

The lizard's scaly skin is generally thick and tough to provide protection. Lizards' scales come in various shapes and sizes. In many species, the scales generally are large and often rough to the touch. In others, the scales are small and smooth. While most species have overlapping scales, others have scales that just touch each other. Some lizard species, such as iguanas, have modified scales that form spines. Others, such as the Namib plated lizard, have bony plates beneath their scales to add strength.

This Komodo dragon (*Varanus komodoensis*) hatchling is breaking out of its shell. The Komodo dragon female lays twenty to twenty-five eggs, each of which is twice the size of a chicken egg. The eggs usually hatch after about nine months.

Life cycle

Most lizards lay eggs, although the females of a few species retain the eggs within their body and give birth to live young. Well-developed young are born ready to take care of themselves.

The suborder Lacertilia is divided into four superfamilies: iguanas and chameleons; geckos; skinks and wall lizards; and monitors.

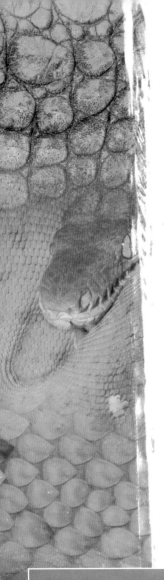

IGUANAS AND CHAMELEONS (IGUANIA)

Iguanas and chameleons make up a large superfamily that is divided into three families: iguanas; agamids; and chameleons. These animals comprise a diverse group of lizards that vary in shape, size, and color.

Physical features

One of the main differences between iguanas, agamas, and chameleons is their teeth. Most iguanas have teeth attached to sockets on the inside of their jaw. These teeth are not replaced when lost. Agamids and chameleons both have acrodont teeth—which means that their teeth are firmly attached to the jawbone instead of in sockets.

Iguanas

About seven hundred species of iguanas are found in North and South America and on many islands, such as Madagascar and the Fiji Islands. Most are either terrestrial or arboreal, but some live near the ocean. Marine iguanas of the Galápagos Islands have webbed feet and a flattened tail. They live on the coast, where they feed on algae in the water. Other iguanas live in deserts. One of their adaptations is the ability to become a lighter color during the day to reflect heat. Some iguanas develop bright colors during the breeding season, such as a bright red or blue throat and abdomen.

The thorny devil (*Moloch horridus*) is a type of agamid found in the Australian desert. It is covered in protective, spiny lumps. Tiny channels between its scales direct dew or rain toward its mouth.

Agamids or chisel-teeth lizards

Agamids are found in Africa, Asia, and Australia. There are about four hundred twenty species. Most have a large head with a thick, fleshy tongue, a cylindrical body, and a fragile tail.

These lizards are diurnal. They hunt for small animals, such as insects. Many male agamids have breeding colors to attract females. They bob their head up and down in front of the female during courtship.

Chameleons

Chameleons are found across Africa, in southern Europe, and across Asia to India and Sri Lanka. They have a long, generally narrow, flattened body. Their head is pointed, with large eyes that can move independently. Instead of a fragile tail, chameleons have a prehensile tail that can wrap around branches. Chameleons are arboreal and adapted to life in trees. They move slowly along branches, gripping firmly with their long toes and tail. This slow movement makes a chameleon difficult to spot, especially when its skin color matches its surroundings.

This Jackson's chameleon (*Chamaeleo jacksonii*) has caught a grasshopper with its long, sticky tongue. Researchers have calculated that a chameleon's tongue shoots out at speeds of more than twenty-six body lengths per second—the equivalent of 13 miles (22 kilometers) per hour. Chameleons can catch prey as far away as 1.5 body lengths.

GECKOS (GEKKOTA)

Geckos are nocturnal lizards well known for their calls and their ability to run up walls. They are found in North and South America, Africa, Asia, and Australia.

The superfamily Gekkota contains more than nine hundred thirty species divided into four families: eyelid geckos; geckos; Southwest Pacific geckos; and flap-footed lizards.

Shared features

Geckos are small, slender lizards, with a large, flat head. Their eyes are relatively large and, as in snakes, are protected by a spectacle scale. Geckos do not have eyelids, so they use their long tongue to wipe dirt off the surface of the eye. Soft scales cover their bodies.

Running up walls

Climbing geckos have specialized feet that allow them to run up walls and across ceilings. Their toes have enlarged pads with overlapping scales underneath. Each of these scales has thousands of tiny hairs. The hairs form a temporary bond with the surface on which the gecko is walking, which is broken when the foot is lifted.

A gecko's foot is covered with millions of minuscule hairs, called setae, with tiny pads at their tips. The feet do not pick up dirt because the setae repel any dirt particles.

When threatened, the leaf-tail gecko (*Uroplatus fimbriatus*) lifts its tail and opens its mouth wide to display its bright-red tongue.

KEY CHARACTERISTICS
GEKKOTA

- **Vertical pupils.**
- **Hairs on toes for gripping.**
- **Spectacle scales.**

Behavior

Although most geckos are nocturnal, some are diurnal. Nocturnal geckos feed on a range of small animals, from insects and spiders to small snakes, birds, and even mammals. Diurnal geckos eat fruit and pollen, too. All geckos find their prey using sight and smell.

Geckos are very noisy lizards. They make a range of sounds from their well-developed larynx (voice box), including chirps, clicks, and growls. Male geckos are territorial and make sounds to warn off other males.

Life cycle

Most female geckos lay only one or two eggs. The eggs usually have hard shells, but a few species lay eggs with soft shells. The young use a special egg tooth on the top of their nose to break out of the egg. Some species of geckos give birth to live young.

SKINKS (SCINCIDAE)

Together with wall and sand lizards, skinks are small lizards that belong to the superfamily Scinomorpha. The family contains more than fourteen hundred species found in a wide variety of habitats worldwide—except the northern regions of Russia, Canada, Alaska, and Antarctica.

Shared features

Most skinks have a cylindrical body and short legs. They range in size from a few inches (cm) to 20 inches (50 cm) long. Their scales are generally smooth and overlap each other. Most have a relatively small, wedge-shaped head. A few species, such as blind burrowing skinks, have either very small limbs or no limbs at all. Blind burrowing skinks spend their lives underground feeding on insects. Their bodies are covered in small scales. They move by "swimming" through the soil or sand.

Most skinks are diurnal and insectivorous, feeding on a range of insects. Some are omnivores. For example, the blue-tongued skink feeds on fruits, flowers, snails, and birds' eggs, as well as insects. The Solomon Islands skink, however, is herbivorous, and feeds solely on plant material.

When threatened, the northern blue-tongued skink (*Tiliqua scincoides intermedia*) opens its mouth to show off its blue tongue. If the threat does not go away, the skink may hiss and flatten its body, making itself look bigger.

Egg layers

Most skinks lay eggs. Some lay just a single egg, while others lay clutches of thirty or more. Most species lay their eggs and leave them. A few species, such as five-lined skinks, look after their eggs. The parent skinks turn each egg regularly to move the embryo inside and prevent it from sticking to one side of the eggshell.

The female broad-headed skink (*Eumeces laticeps*) lays six to sixteen eggs between May and July under logs or in leaf litter. The eggs hatch after about one month.

A few species, such as the Solomon Islands skink, give birth to live young. The Brazilian skink exhibits a unique feature. Female Brazilian skinks retain tiny eggs inside their bodies. The eggs lack a yolk, so the embryo gets its food directly from its mother via a placenta-like structure—an internal nourishing organ similar to that which forms in mammals during gestation. The gestation period for skinks lasts almost one year.

KEY CHARACTERISTICS
SCINCIDAE

- **Small, wedge-shaped heads.**
- **Generally smooth, overlapping scales.**
- **Cylindrical body with a long, "fragile" tail.**
- **Round pupils.**

Some skinks, such as the shingleback, may live up to twenty years. Male and female shinglebacks form pairs that stay together for many years. The pairs separate after mating, but find each other again at the beginning of each breeding season.

WALL AND SAND LIZARDS (LACERTIDAE)

Wall and sand lizards belong to the family Lacertidae. They are closely related to skinks and belong to the same superfamily: Scinomorpha. About two hundred species are found across Africa, Europe, and much of Asia.

Shared features

Wall and sand lizards are relatively small, up to about 10 inches (25 cm) in length. Most have a conical-shaped head, with a pointed snout and a fold of skin across the throat. Their feet have long digits that are suited to running over sand or climbing. Small scales cover the upper surface of their body and large rectangular scales cover the lower surface. Their tail is particularly long and fragile. Unlike the skinks, wall and sand lizards have eyes with movable eyelids. The tongue is long and narrow, with a deep fork at the tip.

Wall and sand lizards are mostly terrestrial. They are active during the day, feeding on invertebrate animals such as insects. They also will tackle small lizards, snakes, and even small mammals.

During early spring and late autumn, the viviparous, or common, lizard (*Lacerta vivipara*) spends a lot of time basking in the Sun. In the morning, its body temperature is about 59 °F (15 °Celsius). It needs to warm up to about 86 °F (30 °C) to become active. It does not bask as much in summer because temperatures are warmer.

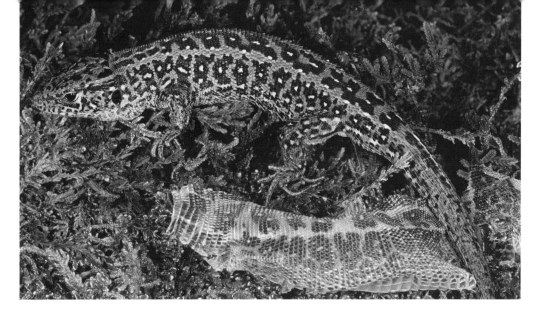

This male sand lizard (*Lacerta agilis*) has just shed its skin. During the breeding season, the males have bright-green sides. The female lays eggs in burrows dug in the sand.

Life cycle

Most wall and sand lizards lay eggs. The viviparous lizard, which lives above the Arctic Circle, is the only lizard to give birth to live young. Egg-layers cannot survive so far north because it is too cold for them to incubate their eggs. Viviparous lizards avoid this problem by keeping their eggs inside their bodies and giving birth to up to eleven live young at a time.

Male sand lizards develop breeding colors and perform courtship displays to attract females. The males often fight over females, threatening each other at first by moving their head up and down. They also can flatten their bodies to look larger. Sand lizards use simple sounds, such as clicks, to attract females and defend their territory.

KEY CHARACTERISTICS
LACERTIDAE

- Small, conical head with a pointed snout.
- Feet with long digits.
- Fold of skin across the throat.
- Long, "fragile" tail.

Surviving in deserts

Many wall and sand lizards live in dry habitats, such as deserts, where they have adapted to the lack of water. Desert-dwelling lizards have fringes at the ends of their toes to help them run on the sand. The shovel-snouted lizard of the Namib Desert in southwest Africa finds food on the surface of sand dunes. It buries itself in the sand when threatened by predators or to escape the high daytime temperatures. While hunting, this lizard often will keep two of its legs raised to avoid the hot sand and to allow cooler air to circulate around its body.

MONITORS (ANGUIMORPHA)

Monitors include some of the largest lizards, such as the impressive Komodo dragon and the only poisonous lizard, the Gila monster. These lizards are found mostly in the tropics, but they also live in Europe, the Middle East, and parts of central South and North America. They live in a variety of habitats, from deserts to tropical rain forests.

Anguimorpha is a large superfamily of one hundred seventy-five species divided into five families: anguids; xenosaurs; beaded lizards; Bornean earless monitors; and monitor lizards.

Shared features
Monitors have rectangular scales covering their bodies, and some have skin folds along their sides. Most have four legs, but a few, such as the slowworm, are legless. All monitors have movable eyelids, and all but the Bornean earless monitors have external ear openings. Most species, particularly the slowworm (also called the blindworm) have fragile tails.

Anguids
Anguid lizards are found in deserts, grasslands, and forests. Some are active during the day, but others are nocturnal. Alligator lizards are found in tropical rain forests, high up in the canopy. They have a long, prehensile

The slowworm (*Anguis fragilis*) may look like a snake, but it is actually a legless lizard that belongs to the anguid family. Even though it can see, it is often called the blindworm because of its tiny eyes.

The Komodo dragon (*Varanus komodoensis*) is the largest lizard in the world. When attacking large prey such as goats, this lizard attacks the feet and lower legs, inflicting terrible bites as it tries to pull the animal down.

tail that wraps around branches to provide a firm grip. Alligator lizards are often brightly colored. The California legless lizards are burrowing lizards found in sandy soils. Able to detect their prey from vibrations, they quickly come to the surface, grab the prey, and disappear again.

Monitor lizards

Monitor lizards usually have a long neck and a narrow head, a long, forked tongue, and a muscular tail that cannot be detached. The Komodo dragon is the largest monitor lizard. It grows up to 10 feet (3 m) long, including the tail. The Komodo dragon has wide jaws, a fold of skin on its neck, and incredibly long, sharp claws. It uses its long, muscular tail as a prop when standing on its hind legs. The tail also is used as a weapon. A Komodo dragon uses its keen sense of smell to find both live prey and the decaying remains of animals. Its saliva contains poisonous bacteria. Prey animals that don't die immediately from bites often die later from an infected bite wound.

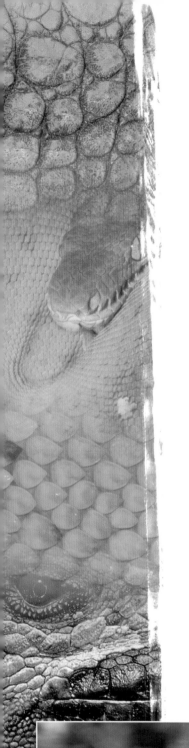

CROCODILIANS (CROCODYLIA)

Crocodilians are the largest living reptiles. They belong to an ancient order of reptiles that is more closely related to dinosaurs than other reptiles. One of the reasons crocodilians have survived for millions of years is that they are highly successful predators.

The order Crocodylia contains twenty-three species divided between three families: alligators; crocodiles; and gharials. Crocodilians range in size from Cuvier's dwarf caiman, at about 5 feet (1.5 m) long, to the Indo-Pacific crocodile, which grows to a massive 23 feet (7 m) long.

Shared features

All crocodilians have a similar body shape—wide and flattened, with the head held out in front and the legs held out to the sides. Their flattened, muscular tails are an efficient shape for swimming. Most have a long snout. Their nostrils are positioned on top of the head so they stay just above the water's surface while the rest of the body is submerged. Crocodilians have a transparent third eyelid, called a nictitating membrane, that protects the eyes when they dive. Their scales are large and bony with raised ridges, giving excellent protection. Instead of molting like snakes, crocodilians shed their scales one at a time. A flap of skin, called a false palate, in their mouth closes off the trachea (windpipe) so they can feed underwater without risk of drowning. Their ears are covered by flaps that close to prevent water from entering when they are submerged.

Morelet's crocodile (*Crocodylus moreletii*) is one of the smaller crocodile species, reaching about 10 feet (3 m) in length. It lives in Central America.

All three types of crocodilians have adapted to a semi-aquatic life, living in and near water. Some have even moved into saltwater. All species of crocodilians lay their eggs on land.

Alligators

The alligator family includes alligators and caimans. They all live in North and South America, except for the Chinese alligator, which lives in eastern China. Their snout is broad and blunt. The teeth on their lower jaw lie inside their mouth and are not visible when the mouth is closed.

Crocodiles

Crocodiles live mainly in Asia and Africa, but some are found in Florida, the Caribbean, and Central and South America. Some species have a long, slender snout, while others have a broad and short snout. The fourth tooth on either side of the lower jaw of crocodiles sticks out when the mouth is closed.

Gharials

Gharials are found in India, Nepal, Pakistan, and Bangladesh. Their body looks just like an alligator, but their snout is very different. It is elongated and flattened, and in males, it ends with a bulbous tip. The shape of their snout makes it easier for gharials to catch fish. They swing their head from side to side so that the snout acts like a trap, catching many fish at once.

The long, thin snout with its bulbous tip is one of the main characteristics of gharials, such as this male Indian gharial (*Gavialis gangeticus*). The gharial's name comes from the Indian word *ghara*, which means "rounded pot."

KEY CHARACTERISTICS
CROCODYLIA

- **Head held out horizontally in front of the body.**
- **Snout with nostrils lying on top.**
- **Large, bony scales.**
- **Muscular, flattened tail.**

The female Nile crocodile (*Crocodylus niloticus*) lays twenty-five to one hundred eggs, which she covers with sand. The young crocodiles hatch about three months later.

Life cycle

All crocodilians lay eggs. The females lay their eggs on land in nests made from plant material or mud. The adults, especially the females, stay close to the nest to guard the eggs from predators, such as monitor lizards and baboons. All the eggs in the nest hatch at the same time. Often, the hatchlings need help leaving the nest, expecially if the mud is dried and hard. The parent crocodiles give considerable care to their hatchlings. Both adults often stay close to the hatchlings for several weeks or even months. The adults respond quickly to their hatchlings' cries of distress. Saltwater crocodiles are particularly aggressive when defending their eggs and hatchlings.

Getting older

Crocodilians become sexually mature (able to mate) once they reach a certain age and size. Their size is just as important as their age, because a crocodile that is not large enough will not be able to mate, even if it is old enough. Like turtles, a crocodilian's sex is determined by the temperature of the environment during the development of the egg (*see page 11*). Crocodilians continue growing throughout their entire life span—even after reaching sexual maturity.

Territories

Adult male crocodilians are territorial. They mark their territory by loudly slapping their heads or snapping their jaws on the surface of the water. The larger, older males are often the dominant animals. They have the largest territories with the best nesting sites and basking areas. The territories of some males also may include the nesting sites of several females. Fights between crocodilians are rare, but occasionally occur between males of the same size that are competing for dominance. When two male crocodilians fight, they line up next to each other facing opposite directions and bang the sides of their heads together.

SOUNDS

Crocodilians make a range of sounds. Hatchlings call to the adults when in danger. They also are very vocal while being fed. The sounds of the hatchlings or adults help keep the hatchlings together. Adult crocodilians also communicate with other adults. The most common adult sound is a loud, low roar, which is repeated and may be echoed by other adults as a way of staying in touch.

Nile crocodiles (*Crocodylus niloticus*) take great care of their eggs. This adult helps a young crocodile hatch by gently cracking its eggshell.

Hunting

Crocodilians are fearsome predators. They are capable of short bursts of high speed to catch prey, but they cannot keep up the chase for long, so they must rely on surprising prey. Most hunt by lying concealed underwater and waiting for prey to approach. Some crocodilians drift slowly in the water, with only the tips of their eyes showing. Caimans use their long tail to trap fish in shallow water. Crocodilians usually are solitary animals, but when a lot of food is available, they sometimes gather and hunt together. This happens during the annual migration of wildebeest in Africa, when thousands of animals cross the Mara River in Kenya.

Each year during their annual migration, thousands of wildebeest cross the Mara River in Kenya. Nile crocodiles (*Crocodylus niloticus*) lie in wait in the water and grab animals as they swim across.

Crocodile food

Crocodilians are opportunistic hunters. They eat whatever they can catch. Most eat insects, tadpoles, frogs, snails, crabs, shrimps, birds, and small fish. They also eat snakes, turtles, and bats. The larger species, such as the Nile and saltwater crocodiles, will tackle mammals, while the caiman will attack anacondas, a type of large snake. All crocodilians have strong jaw muscles for biting and holding their prey. Usually, the prey animal is drowned and then swallowed head first—either whole or in chunks.

Storing fat

Crocodilians convert more than half the food they eat into fat, which is stored in their tail and back. These fat stores are used during times when the animals cannot find prey. A study of Nile crocodiles indicated that they eat only about fifty meals a year—they are able to survive for long periods without any food. Some of the larger crocodilians may survive for up to two years between meals.

DIGESTION

The crocodilian stomach is the most acidic of any vertebrate, which is why crocodiles can digest more than most predators—including the bones and shells of prey animals. A muscular gizzard (a sac containing stones that help break down food) in their stomach aids digestion.

Keeping cool

Crocodilians bask in the Sun during the day to raise their body temperature and return to the water to cool off. They cool off by opening their mouths and exposing their large tongues, from which water can evaporate. Often, crocodilians avoid the hot Sun by remaining underwater or in mud during the day. Many crocodiles lie in the Sun after eating because the heat speeds up digestion.

Caimans are native to South America. This spectacled caiman (*Caiman crocodilus*) holds a piranha in its jaws. *Caiman* is a Spanish word that means "alligator."

UNDER THREAT

Reptile species are under threat all over the world. Habitat loss, poaching, water pollution, and global warming all contribute to the problem.

Habitat loss

Many turtle habitats are being destroyed by tourism. Turtles return to traditional breeding beaches to lay their eggs. Often, these are the same beaches used by tourists who stay in nearby hotels. The disturbance from the tourists and from the hotel lights prevents the turtles from laying their eggs, which contributes to their decline. Also, in many parts of the world, turtle eggs are considered a delicacy.

Terrestrial reptiles, especially snakes and lizards that live in tropical rain forests, also are losing their habitats. Rain forests are being cleared at an ever-increasing rate to make room for farming and new houses. Habitats are being polluted, too. Sewage, oil, and other chemicals pollute the lakes, rivers, and oceans where reptiles live. As the human population increases, people move into new areas and come into contact with snakes, particularly in India. Often, snakes are killed because they are poisonous and could harm people.

Killed for their skin

Many reptiles, including sea kraits, alligators, crocodiles, and caimans, are hunted for their skins. The skins are used to make handbags, briefcases, and shoes. This also contributes to the drastic reduction in the numbers of some species.

Snakeskin is used to make a wide range of clothes, shoes, and bags. Some skins come from legally farmed snakes, but a thriving illegal trade is endangering the survival of some wild snake species.

These reseachers remove the eggs from the nest of a loggerhead turtle (*Caretta caretta*) on a beach in Queensland, Australia. The eggs will be incubated and the hatchlings released. Biologists hope to help more hatchlings survive using this method.

Saving reptiles

Not all reptiles are declining in number. The number of saltwater crocodiles in northern Australia has risen to more than seventy-five thousand from almost nothing because of hunting controls introduced in 1971. Many turtle breeding beaches in Australia, Malaysia, and Indonesia are now protected. Often the eggs are removed and hatched in captivity to increase the number of hatchlings released into the ocean. By carefully controlling the temperature at which the eggs develop, biologists can produce more female turtles—which will help boost future turtle populations.

SNAKE SKIN

Sea kraits (*see page 21*) have been wiped out in the oceans around many small, tropical islands because their skin makes high-quality leather, and they are easy to catch. Scientists believe that if the numbers of sea kraits killed were more carefully controlled, they would maintain their population, and some hunting still could occur.

REPTILE CLASSIFICATION

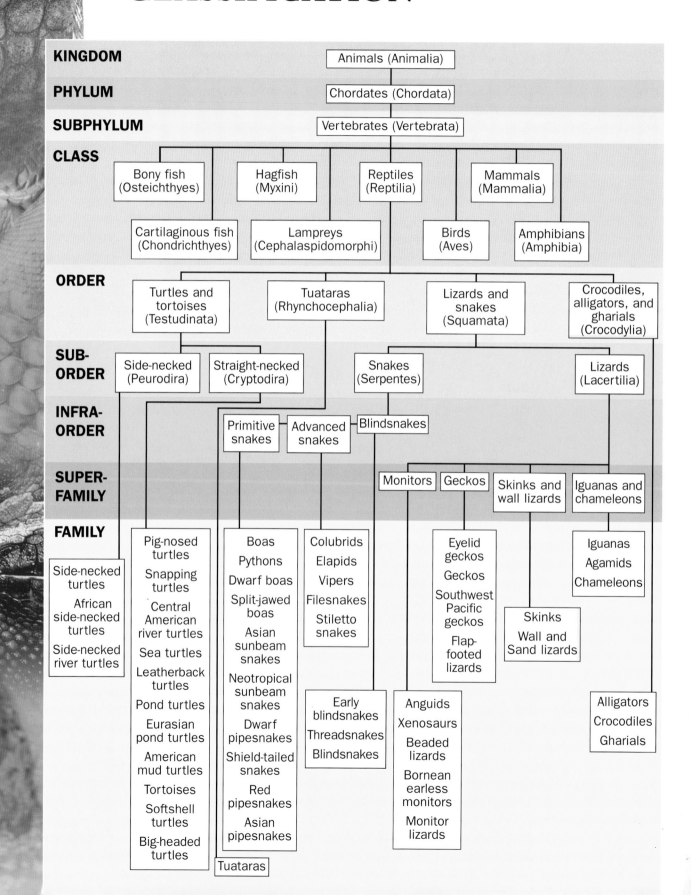

KINGDOM — Animals (Animalia)

PHYLUM — Chordates (Chordata)

SUBPHYLUM — Vertebrates (Vertebrata)

CLASS
- Bony fish (Osteichthyes)
- Cartilaginous fish (Chondrichthyes)
- Hagfish (Myxini)
- Lampreys (Cephalaspidomorphi)
- Reptiles (Reptilia)
- Birds (Aves)
- Mammals (Mammalia)
- Amphibians (Amphibia)

ORDER
- Turtles and tortoises (Testudinata)
- Tuataras (Rhynchocephalia)
- Lizards and snakes (Squamata)
- Crocodiles, alligators, and gharials (Crocodylia)

SUB-ORDER
- Side-necked (Peurodira)
- Straight-necked (Cryptodira)
- Snakes (Serpentes)
- Lizards (Lacertilia)

INFRA-ORDER
- Primitive snakes
- Advanced snakes
- Blindsnakes

SUPER-FAMILY
- Monitors
- Geckos
- Skinks and wall lizards
- Iguanas and chameleons

FAMILY

Side-necked turtles:
- Side-necked turtles
- African side-necked turtles
- Side-necked river turtles

Straight-necked (Cryptodira):
- Pig-nosed turtles
- Snapping turtles
- Central American river turtles
- Sea turtles
- Leatherback turtles
- Pond turtles
- Eurasian pond turtles
- American mud turtles
- Tortoises
- Softshell turtles
- Big-headed turtles

Primitive snakes:
- Boas
- Pythons
- Dwarf boas
- Split-jawed boas
- Asian sunbeam snakes
- Neotropical sunbeam snakes
- Dwarf pipesnakes
- Shield-tailed snakes
- Red pipesnakes
- Asian pipesnakes

Advanced snakes:
- Colubrids
- Elapids
- Vipers
- Filesnakes
- Stiletto snakes

Blindsnakes:
- Early blindsnakes
- Threadsnakes
- Blindsnakes

Monitors:
- Anguids
- Xenosaurs
- Beaded lizards
- Bornean earless monitors
- Monitor lizards

Geckos:
- Eyelid geckos
- Geckos
- Southwest Pacific geckos
- Flap-footed lizards

Skinks and wall lizards:
- Skinks
- Wall and Sand lizards

Iguanas and chameleons:
- Iguanas
- Agamids
- Chameleons

Crocodylia:
- Alligators
- Crocodiles
- Gharials

Tuataras:
- Tuataras

44

GLOSSARY

abdomen the part of the body between the chest and the pelvic girdle (hips), often called the belly.

acrodont an animal with teeth fused to the jaw.

adapted changed according to the surrounding environmental conditions.

aquatic living in water.

autotomy the breaking off of a lizard's tail, usually as a method of defense.

camouflage colors and patterns that allow an animal to blend in with its background.

canopy the uppermost branching layer of a forest.

carapace the protective upper shell of a turtle, made up of large, bony plates.

carnivorous the tendency to hunt and eat other animals.

class a group of related organisms more specific than a phylum but less specific than an order.

cloaca a chamber into which the digestive, urinary, and reproductive systems empty that opens to the outside of the body through the anus.

clutch a set of eggs usually laid by one animal and incubated at the same time.

constriction the method by which some snakes wrap their bodies around prey, squeezing tighter and tighter until they crush or suffocate their victim.

courtship behavior between a male and female animal before mating.

dislocate to force a bone out of its normal position.

diurnal active during the day instead of at night.

ectothermic cold-blooded; having a body temperature that rises and falls with the surrounding temperature.

egg tooth a temporary tooth that reptiles have at the tip of their snouts to break through their leathery eggshell.

embryo an early stage of a vertebrate's development before birth.

estivation a metabolic state similar to hibernation. Some reptiles are inactive in summer to avoid hot weather or drought or in winter to avoid cold weather and to conserve energy.

evolution changes that occur in living organisms over a series of generations and a long period of time.

gestation the time of development from fertilization to birth.

gizzard part of the stomach containing small stones that are used to grind up food into a paste for digestion.

habitat the natural environment or home of a plant or animal.

herbivore an animal that eats plants.

incubate to keep eggs warm and at the correct temperature for development.

invertebrates animals without a backbone; for example, insects.

mammal a vertebrate animal that is covered in hair and whose young are fed milk produced by the female.

metabolism the chemical processes occurring within a living cell or organism that are necessary for the maintenance of life.

migration a seasonal journey between two different locations.

GLOSSARY

molting the process by which animals grow new skin or feathers to replace existing skin or feathers.

nocturnal active at night.

omnivore an animal that eats both animals and plants.

order a group of related organisms with shared characteristics more specific than a class but less specific than a family.

pectoral girdle bones that help form the shoulders.

pelvic girdle bones that help form the hips.

phylum a main division of a kingdom, less specific than a class.

placenta an organ that develops in some female animals during pregnancy, through which the mother nourishes the developing young.

plastron the underside of a turtle shell, made of many bony plates.

poaching illegal hunting.

predator an animal that catches and kills other animals for food.

prehensile adapted for seizing, grasping, or holding, especially by wrapping around an object.

prey an animal that is caught and killed by a predator for food.

rain forests dense forests with high levels of precipitation and a huge variety of plants and animals.

retina the lining of the eye on which the light falls to help form an image, like the film in a camera.

scales a covering of platelike structures on reptiles that provides protection from predators.

sp. an abbreviation for "species," used in the Latin binomial classification name for a plant or animal whose exact species is unknown.

spectacle scale a transparent scale that covers and protects the eye.

spur a small, bony outgrowth.

streamlined having a shape that moves easily through air and water.

suffocate to stop an animal from breathing, usually by using pressure.

superfamily an intermediate classification of organisms that falls between a suborder and a family.

temperate a moderate climate that lacks extremes in temperature.

terrestrial ground-dwelling.

translucent nearly—but not completely—transparent; light can still come through.

tropical parts of the world just north and south of the equator; a hot, wet climate.

uncinate something that is bent at the end like a hook.

venom the poisonous secretion of an animal; used to kill prey or as a defense against predators.

vertebrate an animal with a backbone; for example, fish, amphibians, reptiles, and mammals.

viviparous able to give birth to live offspring.

webbed feet having skin connecting the toes; helpful for swimming.

FURTHER INFORMATION

BOOKS

Behler, John L. *Reptiles. National Audubon Society First Field Guides.* Scholastic (1999).

Dennard, Deborah. *Snakes. Our Wild World* (series). Northword Press (2003).

DK Animal Encyclopedia. DK Publishing (2000).

Ganeri, Anita. *Animal Groupings. Nature Files* (series). Chelsea House (2004).

Halliday, Tim & Kraig Adler, eds. *The New Encyclopedia of Reptiles & Amphibians.* Oxford University Press (2002).

McCarthy, Colin. *Reptile. Eyewitness Books* (series). DK Publishing (2000).

Miller, Ruth. *Reptiles. Animal Kingdom* (series). Raintree (2005).

O'Shea, Mark. *Smithsonian Handbooks: Reptiles and Amphibians.* DK Publishing (2002).

Royston, Angela. *Reptiles. Living Nature* (series). Chrysalis Children's Books (2004).

Spilsbury, Richard and Louise A. *Classifying Living Things: Classifying Reptiles.* Heinemann Library (2003).

Swinburne, Stephen R. *Turtle Tide: The Ways of Sea Turtles.* Boyds Mills Press (2005).

Wallace, Holly. *Classification. Life Processes* (series). Heinemann Library (2002).

Winner, Cherie. *Everything Reptile: What Kids Really Want to Know About Reptiles. Kids FAQs* (series). Northword Press (2004).

WEB SITES

http://animaldiversity.ummz.umich.edu/site/accounts/information/Reptilia.html
Explore the reptile pages of the University of Michigan's animal diversity Web site.

http://nationalzoo.si.edu/ConservationAndScience/AquaticEcosystems/SeaTurtles/
Learn what you can do to help save sea turtles and why they are so important.

www.arkive.org/species/GES/reptiles/
Get facts and images on forty-eight different reptiles.

www.enchantedlearning.com/subjects/reptiles/printouts.shtml
Choose your favorite animal from a range of reptiles and discover what makes it special.

www.kingsnake.com/oz/
Discover which reptiles live in Australia; includes maps and notes on individual species.

www.rit.edu/~rhrsbi/GalapagosPages/Reptiles.html
Take a trip to the Galápagos Islands and meet some unique reptiles.

www.sandiegozoo.org/animalbytes/a-reptiles.html
Meet the reptiles of the San Diego Zoo and follow the links to some fascinating facts.

INDEX

Page numbers in **bold** refer to a photograph or illustration.